All Souped Up

✦✧✖✦✖✦✧✖✦✧✖✦✖✦✧✖

Recipes

from

All Stitched Up

Carolyn Dowie & Shelagh Martell

ISBN 978-1-927931-05-9

Cover and book design by Vivalogue Ltd

Front cover panel designed and stitched by Shelagh Martell
Photographed by Mark Wilkinson Photography

Printed in the United Kingdom by
Martins the Printers, Berwick-upon-Tweed

Notes for Cooks

FOR all recipes, seasoning is with salt and freshly
ground black pepper to taste.
CONSISTENCY of soups can be varied with the addition of extra stock, depending on your preference.

Table of Contents

About All Stitched Up

CAROLYN DOWIE & SHELAGH MARTELL are friends who live in the North East of England. On one occasion Carolyn admired the petit point evening bag that Shelagh had and they fell into talking about tapestry and stitching, interests they both shared. Carolyn had been asked by Anna Pearson, a well-known needlepoint designer, about becoming a representative for her work in the North East. She thought it would be much more fun to do this with someone else. Thus was born All Stitched Up.

We started by holding an Open Day in the Tyne Valley in 2000. As there was considerable interest, we decided to start holding regular stitching sessions where people could get together and stitch, and we could provide not only materials but also advice, tuition and encouragement. We also hold regular classes in Edinburgh and North Yorkshire.

We now offer a large selection of designs by Anna Pearson and others, which range from simple bargello patterns to complicated stitchery pieces. Each design comes in three or four standard colourways. However, the unique feature of our service is that we can tailor any design to suit a client's particular décor.

In August 2009, we took over the management and marketing of Anna Pearson's designs, and updated and expanded the website, *www.needle-point.co.uk*. We produce two or three new designs each year with the help of our networkers around the country. We also offer a range of painted canvases for those who enjoy petit point. These are painted by well-known Northumbrian artist Sarah Blackett-Ord. She carefully matches her colours to Appleton wools.

Each kit comes with a taped canvas, needles, all wools and threads needed and full colour computer generated instructions with easy-to-follow diagrams of all the stitches. Some kits use wool only, others use a mixture of wool, cottons and variegated hand-dyed silks.

We have a number of representatives around the country who hold classes themselves, sell our designs and teach their students. See page 130 for details of our classes and networkers.

www.needle-point.co.uk 01434 672 389

Open Days

This Darsham Rug was on display at an Open Day in Dorset in 2012. This rug is worked in squares and can therefore be made to any size and shape. It also comes as a kit to make an attractive Florentine cushion. Colours can be matched to your own interior colour scheme. This particular rug was stitched by Harriet Benson in Northumberland.

Vegetable Soups

Roast beetroot and apple soup

- 600g raw beetroot, peeled and quartered
- 2 onions, peeled and thinly sliced
- 2 sprigs of thyme
- 2 large apples, peeled, cored and chopped
- vegetable oil spray
- 1 litre vegetable or chicken stock
- flat leaf parsley, chopped

PREHEAT oven to 200°C/gas mark 6.

PUT the beetroot, onion, thyme and apple in a roasting tin. Spray with the oil and season. Cover with foil and roast for 30–40 minutes; test with a knife after 30 minutes.

HEAT the stock to a simmer and then add the beetroot, apple and thyme. Bring to the boil.

REMOVE from the heat and remove the sprig of thyme. Whizz until smooth. Adjust seasoning if necessary.

DELICIOUS served hot or cold with a sprinkling of flat leaf parsley.

- Serves 5
- Eating apples are best for this recipe.

Beetroot and cumin soup

- 2 tbsp sunflower oil
- 1 large onion, peeled and roughly chopped
- 2 garlic cloves, peeled and chopped
- 2 tsp ground cumin
- 750g cooked beetroot (not in vinegar)
- 1.5 litres vegetable stock
- 6 tbsp apple juice
- 2 tbsp crème fraîche plus extra to serve
- cumin seeds, lightly toasted

HEAT the sunflower oil in a large saucepan. Add the onion and garlic and fry for 5 minutes. At the same time, bring the stock to boil in another saucepan.

CHOP the beetroot coarsely.

STIR the ground cumin into the onion and garlic and add the beetroot. Pour in the stock and boil for 5 minutes. Take off the heat.

ADD the apple juice and stir in the 2 tbsp of crème fraîche. Liquidise until smooth. Taste and adjust seasoning with salt and pepper.

GARNISH with a swirl of crème fraîche and the toasted cumin seeds.

- Serves 6
- The cumin really lifts the taste of this soup.

Beetroot soup with dill and horseradish cream

- 1 bunch beetroot, approx 700g
- 2 tbsp olive oil
- 1 onion, diced
- 1 stick of celery, diced
- 1 potato (approx 200g), peeled and diced
- 500 ml chicken or vegetable stock
- 2 tsp hot horseradish sauce
- 2 tbsp half-fat crème fraîche
- 1 tbsp chopped dill

PREHEAT the oven to 220°C/gas mark 7.

RINSE and trim the beetroot then chop into 2cm cubes and toss with 1 tbsp oil.

SCATTER onto a foil-lined roasting tin and roast for 20 minutes.

HEAT the remaining oil in a pan and add the onion and the celery. Cook for about 10 minutes until softened. Add the potato, cook for 5 minutes then tip in the roasted beetroot.

ADD the stock and 250ml water. Simmer for 10–15 minutes.

COOL a little then blitz in a blender or with a stick blender until smooth.

REHEAT in the pan adding a little water if it's too thick.

JUST before serving, mix the horseradish and the crème fraîche.

GARNISH with a swirl of the horseradish and crème fraîche mixture into each bowl and sprinkle with the chopped dill.

- Serves 6
- If you don't want such a hot horseradish flavour, use creamed horseradish instead.

Really easy beetroot soup

- 2 large beetroot, approx 725g
- 1 tsp Dijon mustard
- 1 tbsp balsamic vinegar
- buttermilk or yogurt to serve

COVER beetroot with cold water in a pan, bring to the boil and then simmer for 2 hours.

PEEL off the skin and whizz with the mustard and balsamic vinegar, adding boiling liquid as needed to achieve the consistency you want.

SERVE with a swirl of buttermilk or yogurt.

- Serves 5
- This is equally good served hot or cold.

Sampler by Valerie

Designed by Valerie Hand. This is a traditional sampler which will enable the stitcher to learn many new and interesting stitches using wool throughout. Valerie

designed it as a teaching project for her students. The central star can be replaced with initials if desired.

It will soon be available on 18 mesh.

Broccoli and basil soup

- 1 large white onion, peeled
- 1 large potato, peeled
- 3 celery sticks
- 2 tbsp olive oil, plus extra to drizzle
- 1 head of broccoli, approx 375g
- 2 garlic cloves, peeled and roughly chopped
- 1.3 litres vegetable stock
- 25g pack of fresh basil

CHOP roughly the onion, potato and celery sticks. Heat the oil in a large pan and add the chopped vegetables. Cook, stirring occasionally for 5–10 minutes until the vegetables are translucent but not brown.

PREPARE the broccoli by chopping the stem in small pieces and halving large florets.

ADD the broccoli, garlic and the stock to the pan. Bring to the boil then simmer for 10 minutes or until the vegetables are just cooked through.

ADD the basil (leaves and stalks), saving a few pretty leaves for garnish.

WHIZZ the soup in a blender until really smooth in batches. Reheat and check the seasoning.

DRIZZLE each serving with a little oil and top with the reserved basil leaves.

- Serves 6

Broccoli soup with goat's cheese

- 900g broccoli
- 50g butter
- 1 onion, peeled and roughly chopped
- 1 litre vegetable stock
- 600ml milk
- 85g goat's cheese

CHOP the broccoli keeping stem and florets separate.
MELT the butter and add the onion and the chopped broccoli stem. Soften for 5 minutes then add the broccoli florets, the stock and the milk. Simmer for 8 minutes.
BLEND until smooth.
GARNISH by crumbling the goat's cheese over each serving.

- Serves 4
- A nice serving variation is to make some croûtes by toasting slices of baguette, then topping each slice with some crumbled goat's cheese, grill to melt and then float on the soup.

Broccoli and bacon soup

- 1 medium onion, roughly chopped
- 25g butter
- 200g streaky bacon or lardons
- 3 small potatoes
- 1.5 litres chicken stock
- 300g tenderstem broccoli
- 150ml milk

SOFTEN the onion in the butter in a deep pan. Stir in half the bacon, snipped into small pieces, or the lardons. Reserve some pieces for garnish.

ADD the potatoes and let the flavours blend with as little colouring as possible.

POUR in the stock and bring to the boil, adding salt and freshly ground black pepper. Turn the heat down and simmer for around 15 minutes until the potatoes are really soft.

ADD the broccoli, trimmed of any tough stems, and simmer for 10 minutes. They want to be bright green.

POUR in the milk, simmer briefly, then whizz until smooth. Check the seasoning.

GRILL or fry the reserved bacon or lardons until crisp.

SERVE the soup in heated bowls each with pieces of crisp bacon on top.

- Serves 6

Butternut squash soup with harissa

- 1 butternut squash, approx 600g
- 1 onion, roughly chopped
- 3 tbsp olive oil
- 500ml vegetable stock
- 2 tbsp harissa paste
- crème fraîche or sour cream to serve

PREHEAT oven to 200°C/gas mark 6.

CHOP the squash into large chunks, then add the onions.

TOSS the vegetables with the olive oil, spread on a roasting tin and roast for 20 minutes or until tender.

SCOOP the flesh of the butternut squash out, and whizz with the roasted onions, the vegetable stock and the harissa paste until smooth.

TRANSFER to a saucepan and reheat gently.

SERVE in warm bowls with a swirl of crème fraîche or sour cream.

- Serves 4
- The joy of this soup is that you don't need to peel the butternut squash.

Butternut squash and sage soup

- 1 large butternut squash, peeled
- 2 medium onions, peeled
- 4 garlic cloves, peeled
- 55g unsalted butter
- 1 litre water
- 125ml whipping cream
- 10 large sage leaves, finely sliced

ROUGHLY chop the squash, onions and garlic. Put the vegetables with the butter and 1 tsp salt into a large saucepan. Sweat for about 7 minutes then pour over the water and bring to the boil. Boil for 15 minutes until soft.

LIQUIDISE in a blender and pour back into the saucepan. Add three-quarters of the cream and most of the sage leaves then heat through and season to taste.

LADLE into 6 bowls.

GARNISH with a swirl of cream and a few of the remaining sage leaves.

- Serves 6
- This freezes well without the cream.

Thai butternut squash soup

- 1 onion, chopped
- 2 tbsp vegetable oil
- 1 tbsp Thai green curry paste
- 2 medium butternut squash, peeled
- 500ml chicken stock (use stock cubes or pots)
- 400ml can of coconut milk
- crème fraîche

ROUGHLY chop the squash and the onions. Heat the oil and cook the onions very slowly until transparent. Add the Thai curry paste and continue to cook for a couple of minutes.

ADD the squash, chicken stock and coconut milk and bring to the boil. Simmer until the squash is soft, about 20 minutes.

REMOVE from the heat and allow to cool a little. Whizz until smooth, adding a little water if it is too thick. Check the seasoning.

SERVE in warm bowls with a swirl of crème fraîche.

- Serves 4
- The Thai curry paste and the coconut milk make this a really special soup.

Curried butternut squash, lentil and coconut soup

- 1 tbsp olive oil
- 1 butternut squash
- 200g carrots, diced
- 1 tbsp curry powder
- 100g red lentils
- 700ml vegetable stock
- 1 tin reduced-fat coconut milk
- fresh coriander and naan bread to serve

PREPARE the squash by removing the seeds and membrance and cut into rough chunks.

HEAT the oil in a large saucepan, add the squash and carrots, sizzle 1 minute, then stir in the curry powder and cook for 1 minute more. Tip in the lentils, the vegetable stock and coconut milk and give it all a good stir around.

BRING to the boil and then simmer for about 15 minutes until it is all tender.

USING a hand blender or a food processor, blitz until it is as smooth as you like. Check the seasoning.

GARNISH with a scattering of chopped fresh coriander.

SERVE with warm naan bread.

- Serves 6

No-peel curried butternut squash soup

- 1 butternut squash, halved and seeded
- 2 large onions, peeled and quartered
- 1 medium head of garlic
- 1.4 litres vegetable stock
- 1 bay leaf
- 1 tsp dark brown soft sugar
- 1 tsp curry powder
- ½ tsp dried oregano
- ½ tsp ground cinnamon
- ¼ tsp ground nutmeg
- 225g low-fat natural yogurt

PREHEAT oven to 180°C/gas mark 4 and line a baking tray with baking parchment or foil.

PLACE squash halves and onion into the prepared baking tray. Wrap garlic in foil and place on tray.

ROAST in the centre of the oven for 45 minutes, or a little longer, until squash is tender. Remove from oven and set aside until cool enough to handle.

SQUEEZE the garlic cloves from their skin into the food processor. Scrape the flesh from the squash and add to the food processor along with the onion.

PUREE until smooth. Add some vegetable stock to help make it really smooth.

SCRAPE the purée into a large pot and stir in the vegetable stock. Add the bay leaf, brown sugar, curry powder, oregano, cinnamon, nutmeg, salt and pepper.

BRING to the boil and simmer gently for about 10 minutes. Remove from the heat, remove the bay leaf and stir in the yogurt.

GARNISH with some chopped fresh parsley.

Serves 8

Alice Scheme I

Spiced carrot and parsnip soup with sage

- 1 tbsp each cumin seeds and coriander seeds
- 60g butter
- 1 large onion, peeled and chopped
- 2 garlic cloves, peeled and chopped
- 400g carrots, peeled and chopped
- 400g parsnips, peeled and chopped
- 1.2 litres chicken or vegetable stock
- 1 tbsp olive oil
- 20 or so small fresh sage leaves

TIP the cumin and coriander seeds into a medium frying pan and head them gently until they are fragrant and start to pop. Grind them using a pestle and mortar.

MELT 50g butter in a large saucepan and stir in the onion, garlic and seeds. Cook gently, partially covered, for 10 minutes.

STIR in the carrots and parsnips and season. Pour in the stock and bring to the boil. Simmer for about 20 minutes. Leave to cool a little then liquidise in batches.

HEAT the remaining butter and oil in the frying pan and when it is sizzling fry the sage leaves with a pinch of salt for about 30 seconds.

REHEAT the soup and garnish with crispy sage leaves.

- Serves 6

Spiced carrot and lentil soup

- 2 tsp cumin seeds
- pinch of chilli flakes
- 2 tbsp olive oil
- 600g carrots, washed and coarsely grated
- 140g split red lentils
- 1 litre hot vegetable stock (cube is fine)
- 125ml milk
- plain yogurt and naan bread to serve

HEAT a large saucepan and dry-fry the cumin seeds and chilli flakes for 1 min or until they are fragrant and start to pop. Scoop out about half the seeds with a spoon and set aside.

ADD the oil, carrots, lentils, stock and milk to the pan and bring to the boil. Simmer for 15 minutes until the lentils have swollen and softened.

WHIZZ the soup with a stick blender or in a food processor until smooth (or leave chunky if you prefer). Garnish with a dollop of yogurt and a sprinkling of the reserved seeds and serve with warmed naan bread.

- Serves 4
- Substitute a few teaspoons of harissa paste instead of the chilli and cumin.
- You could add cooked shredded chicken at the end to make the soup more substantial.

Spiced carrot and orange soup

- ½ onion
- 500g diced carrots
- 1 tbsp olive oil
- 600ml vegetable stock (cube is fine)
- Juice and zest of 1 orange
- 1 tsp ground cumin
- natural yogurt to serve

GENTLY heat and soften the onion and carrots in the olive oil in pan for about 15 minutes.

ADD the vegetable stock, the orange juice and zest and the cumin.

SIMMER for 10 minutes until the carrots are tender. Cool a little then liquidise. Reheat and season.

GARNISH with a swirl of yogurt in each bowl.

- Serves 2
- This is a winning flavour combination.

Carrot and ginger soup

- 1 onion, peeled and chopped
- 2 celery sticks, trimmed and chopped
- 2 garlic cloves, peeled and chopped
- 600g carrots, peeled and roughly chopped
- 1cm piece of fresh root ginger, finely grated
- olive oil
- 1 litre chicken stock
- yogurt and snipped chives to serve

COOK the onion, celery, garlic and ginger in the oil for 2–3 minutes.

ADD the stock and the carrots and bring to a boil. Reduce the heat and simmer for 20 minutes until the carrots are tender.

COOL slightly and add salt and pepper. Liquidise until it is the consistency you like.

GARNISH with a swirl of yogurt and a few snipped chives in each bowl.

- Serves 4
- Ginger freezes beautifully as a whole root and can be grated from frozen.

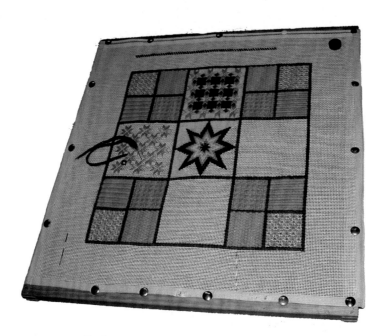

A Work in Progress

Pictured above is our Beatrice tapestry kit, in Scheme IV colours. Beatrice was designed by Anna Pearson on 14 mesh canvas and is an interesting design worked in Crewel Wool and Perle Cotton using a number of different stitches. This design comes in four different standard colourways but we can custom design a colour palette for you to match to your own special interior colour scheme.

Roasted carrot soup with herb crème fraîche

- 1 onion, cut into wedges
- 800g carrots, peeled and roughly chopped
- butter
- 1 bay leaf
- 1 tsp runny honey
- 2 litres vegetable or chicken stock
- 200ml crème fraîche
- 4 tbsp chopped mint, basil and chervil

HEAT the oven to 200°C/gas mark 6.

PUT the onions and carrots in a roasting tin with a few knobs of butter and roast for 30 minutes or until the vegetables are tinged brown.

TIP into a pan and add the bay leaf, honey and stock and bring to a simmer. Cook for about 10 minutes or until the carrots are tender. Remove the bay leaf and allow to cool a little.

WHIZZ until smooth. Season and keep warm.

MIX the crème fraîche and herbs and season well. (Keep a few chopped herbs aside for garnish.)

GARNISH with a dollop of the herb crème fraîche and a few of the reserved herbs.

- Serves 6
- Use any mixture of fresh herbs available.

Carrot soup with melting cheese and chives

- 1 tbsp olive oil
- 2 red onions, peeled and chopped
- 2 garlic cloves, peeled and crushed
- a small handful of rosemary, leaves only
- 6 large carrots, peeled and roughly chopped
- a splash of sherry
- 600ml vegetable stock
- a small handful of chives, snipped
- 100g cheddar cheese, crumbled

HEAT the oil in a large saucepan and gently cook the onion, garlic and rosemary for about 10 minutes or until the onion has softened. Add the carrots and cook for a further 2–3 minutes.

INCREASE the heat and splash in the sherry, allowing it to bubble until it has almost evaporated, then pour in the stock. Bring to the boil and simmer for 20 minutes or until the carrots are softened and beginning to break up.

WHIZZ until smooth. Reheat and season to taste.

GARNISH with the crumbled cheese and some snipped chives. Serve with crusty bread.

- Serves 6

Cauliflower and Stilton soup

- 30g butter
- 1 tbsp olive oil
- 1 leek, thinly sliced
- 1 onion, finely chopped
- 2 garlic cloves, crushed
- 1 cauliflower, approx 1.25kg
- 1 litre chicken or vegetable stock
- 4 sprigs of thyme, leaves only
- 200g Stilton, crumbled
- 250ml milk
- white pepper

MELT the butter and oil in a large saucepan over a medium heat. Add the leek, onion and garlic and cook for about 5 minutes. Chop the cauliflower and add it to the saucepan.

COOK, stirring occasionally, for about 10 minutes until softened. Add the stock and thyme and bring it to the boil. Reduce the heat and simmer for about 25 minutes.

REDUCE the heat to low and add the Stilton. Stir until almost melted, add the milk and gently heat through (do not allow to boil). Season with white pepper.

GARNISH with a swirl of crème fraîche and snipped chives.

- Serves 4

Celeriac and apple soup

- 75g butter
- 2 onions, peeled and chopped
- 2 leeks, trimmed and chopped
- 2 carrots, peeled and chopped
- 1 celery heart, trimmed and sliced
- 1 apple, peeled, cored and diced
- 1 bulb celeriac (900g), peeled and diced
- 200ml cider
- 1.2 litres chicken or vegetable stock

MELT the butter in a large pan over a medium heat. Add the onion, leeks, carrots and celery and cook gently for 12 minutes, stirring occasionally until starting to colour. Add the apple and celeriac to the pan and cook 5 more minutes.

POUR in the cider and cook until well reduced, then add the stock and some seasoning. Bring to the boil then simmer until the celeriac is tender.

WHIZZ the soup and then pass it through a sieve to eliminate the fibrous bits of the vegetables. Check the seasoning and reheat.

- Serves 8–10
- Optional garnish: toast slices of baguette then spread one side with butter; crumble over some Stilton and grill till melted.

Celery and Stilton soup

- 75g butter
- 8 head of celery, trimmed and chopped
- 6 tbsp flour
- 575ml milk
- 1.1 litre chicken stock (2 stock cubes or pots)
- 125g Stilton, crumbled
- croutons and snipped chives to serve

MELT the butter in a saucepan and add the celery. Cook gently until softened.

STIR in the flour and cook gently for a minute to make a roux. Remove from the heat and gradually add the milk and the stock. Bring to the boil and simmer for 10–15 minutes until thickened.

GRADUALLY add the Stilton and stir until melted. Season to taste.

GARNISH with croutons and snipped chives.

- Serves 4
- Leftover Stilton from Christmas freezes well and can be used for soups.

Celery and celeriac soup

- 350g celery, cleaned and chopped
- 50g butter
- 2 small onions, peeled and chopped
- ½ tsp celery salt
- 1 head of celeriac, approx 225g
- 850ml chicken stock
- 150ml double cream

PEEL and chop the celeriac and leave it in acidulated water to prevent browning.

MELT the butter in a large pan and gently cook the celery and onions for about 20 minutes or until softened but not coloured. Add the celery salt. Drain the celeriac and add it to the pan along with the stock.

BRING to the boil and check for seasoning to see if any plain salt is needed. Skim off any scum that may have formed and simmer very gently, covered, for 35–45 minutes.

LIQUIDISE thoroughly, a minute for each batch, as this helps the soup to be really creamy. Finally, push through a sieve into a clean pan. Add the cream and black pepper and reheat.

SERVE sprinkle with croutons.

- Serves 4

Courgette and carrot soup

- 2 medium shallots, chopped
- 1 tbsp oil
- 4 small courgettes, grated
- 225g fresh tomatoes, skinned and chopped
- 900ml chicken stock

FRY the shallot in the oil until transparent.

TOSS the remaining vegetables in with the shallot and add the stock.

SIMMER for 10 minutes then taste and adjust the seasoning. Whizz until smooth.

- Serves 4
- Nice served with hot garlic bread.

Log Cabin Scheme IV

Courgette and green pepper soup

- 30ml oil
- 1 large green pepper, seeded and diced
- 1 small onion, chopped
- 2 leeks, sliced
- 500g courgette, trimmed and sliced
- 1 bay leaf
- 750ml chicken stock
- a few sprigs of parsley
- 45g skimmed milk powder
- 120ml milk

HEAT the oil in a large saucepan and add the green pepper (saving some for garnish), onion and leeks. Cover the saucepan and sweat the vegetables over a low heat until they are softened.

ADD the courgettes and toss them to coat them in the oil. Add the bay leaf, stock, parsley and salt. Cover and simmer for about 20 minutes until softened.

BLEND the milk powder with the milk and add this to the soup. Whizz until smooth and check seasoning.

EITHER reheat without boiling or cool and chill.

SERVE garnished with a sprinkling of chopped green peppers.

- Serves 4–6

Courgette, leek, pea and spinach soup

- 40g butter
- 1 large onion, diced
- 2 garlic cloves, finely chopped
- 3 leeks, thinly sliced
- 3 courgettes, thinly sliced
- 500g frozen peas
- 3 large handfuls of spinach leaves
- 1 litre vegetable stock

MELT the butter and add the onion and garlic. Cook gently for about 10 minutes until softened but not brown.

ADD courgettes and leeks and cook for around 15 minutes until soft.

ADD the stock and frozen peas, bring to the boil and simmer for around 10 minutes.

ADD the spinach leaves and allow to wilt, around 2 minutes.

COOL a little and then whizz. Return to the pan and season well.

SERVE with a dollop of pesto and a swirl of crème fraîche.

- Serves 8

Fennel and courgette soup

- 75g butter
- 1 large onion, diced
- 2 potatoes, peeled and diced
- 2 fennel bulbs, thinly sliced
- 2 garlic cloves, crushed
- 1.75 litres vegetable stock
- 2 courgettes, diced
- large handful rocket leaves
- 100ml double cream
- 200ml crème fraîche
- 2 tbsp freshly grated parmesan

MELT the butter in a large saucepan and add the onion, potatoes, fennel and garlic. Cook for a few minutes to soften, then add the stock. Bring to a simmer and cook for about 10–15 minutes until the fennel is tender. Add the courgettes and rocket and cook for a further 4 or 5 minutes.

ALLOW to cool a little then whizz until very smooth. Stir in the cream, crème fraîche, parmesan and seasoning.

LADLE into warm bowls and serve with lots of chopped fresh parsley and some extra parmesan sprinkled on top.

- Serves 6

Fennel and cauliflower soup

- 40g butter
- 1 tbsp olive oil
- 1 large onion, peeled and chopped
- 3 garlic cloves, peeled and crushed
- 2 large bulbs of fennel, trimmed and sliced
- 1 large cauliflower, cut into florets
- 1 litres chicken or vegetable stock
- 2 bay leaves
- 2 tbsp chopped fresh tarragon
- 100ml double cream (optional)
- 25ml Pernod or pastis (optional)

MELT the butter and oil in a large saucepan. Add the onion and garlic and cook, uncovered, for 10 minutes or until soft. Add the fennel and cauliflower florets and continue to cook.

POUR over the stock and add the bay leaves and tarragon and season well.

BRING to the boil, cover and simmer for 15 minutes or until the cauliflower is soft.

ALLOW to cool a little and then whizz until smooth.

ADD the double cream and Pernod or pastis if desired.

GARNISH with fresh chopped parsley.

- Serves 6

Roasted fennel and cider soup

- 2 large fennel bulbs
- 2 large red onions
- olive oil for drizzling
- 1 bunch thyme (preferably lemon thyme)
- 1 tbsp coriander seeds
- 1 tbsp fennel seeds
- 300ml dry cider
- 300ml double cream
- a splash of apple brandy or Calvados

PREHEAT the oven to 200°C/gas mark 6.

TRIM the feathery leaves off the fennel, reserving some for garnish. Trim the rest of the bulbs, then cut into wedges. Cut the onions into similarly sized wedges then place in a roasting tin with the fennel. Drizzle with oil and scatter over the thyme and the coriander and fennel seeds.

ROAST 30 minutes until lightly caramelised. Test for tenderness and if necessary roast further.

POUR over the cider and then roast a further 15 minutes until almost all the cider has been absorbed.

LEAVE to cool slightly and then whizz until smooth. Return to the saucepan and stir in the stock. Bring to the boil then simmer until reduced by one-third. Leave to cool.

PUSH through a sieve using the back of a wooden

spoon. Pour into a clean pan, add the cream and heat gently, not letting it boil and stirring constantly, until heated through.

ADD the apple brandy or Calvados just before serving.
LADLE into warm bowls and sprinkle a little chopped parsley on each bowl.

- Serves 4–6
- Fennel and cider: a marriage made in heaven!

Coriander Scheme III

Wild garlic soup

- 2 tbsp olive oil
- 1 onion, chopped
- 1 large potato, peeled and roughly chopped
- 1.2 litres chicken stock (3 cubes or stock pots)
- 170g wild garlic leaves

FRY the onion and potato in a large saucepan until softened but not coloured.

ADD the stock (or cubes and water) and bring to the boil. Simmer for 15 minutes or so until the potato is cooked. Check the seasoning—it will need to be well seasoned.

KEEPING a few wild garlic leaves for garnish, add the rest to the soup. Stir until wilted.

WHIZZ until smooth, adding crème fraîche to taste.

CHOP the reserved leaves into fine shreds.

SERVE the soup in warmed bowls with a swirl of crème fraîche and some shredded leaves on each serving. You can also add a pretty white wild garlic flower if you like.

- Serves 6–8
- Wild garlic grows in Shelagh's garden in the same places as snow drops. The leaves are gently garlic flavoured and the pretty white flowers are edible too.

Leek and potato soup with pesto

- 1 large potato, peeled and cubes
- 1 small onion, peeled and chopped
- 2 leeks, trimmed and sliced
- 25g butter
- 600ml vegetable stock
- 300ml semi-skimmed milk
- 1 tbsp pesto

HEAT the butter in a large saucepan and cook the potato, onion and leeks for 5 mins.

ADD the vegetable stock, bring to the boil and simmer for about 15 mins until the vegetables are tender.

COOL slightly and then whizz in a blender until smooth.

RETURN to the pan with the milk and the pesto. Season and reheat.

- Serves 4
- The pesto gives a slight twist to the traditional leek and potato soup. Once the milk and pesto have been added, the soup could be refrigerated and served chilled.

Leek and Stilton soup

- 350g leeks, trimmed, sliced and washed
- 250g Stilton, crumbled, plus extra to serve
- 50g butter
- 2 medium potatoes, peeled & cut into chunks
- 2 bay leaves
- 3 heaped tbsp thick, plain yogurt

CUT the leeks into finger-thick rounds and put them into a deep saucepan with the butter. Cook slowly over a low-to-moderate heat, covered. Stir occasionally. After about 20 minutes they should be soft.

ADD the potatoes to the saucepan with the bay leaves and 1 litre of water and bring to the boil. Turn the heat down to simmer and cook for 20 minutes.

REMOVE the bay leaves, add the crumbled cheese then whizz to a creamy purée. Season, but not much salt will be needed as the Stilton is salty.

SWIRL some yogurt into each bowl and pass a bowl of crumbled Stilton round for those who want extra.

- Serves 4
- Another use for leftover Christmas Stilton.

Leek and split pea soup

- 75g split green peas, rinsed
- 75g streaky bacon, chopped
- 1.1 litres chicken stock
- 700g leeks, trimmed, sliced and washed

COVER the split peas with boiling water and leave to soak for 2 hours. Rinse in several changes of cold water and drain thoroughly.

PUT the bacon in a large saucepan and heat gently until the fat runs out of the bacon.

ADD the split peas, stock and seasoning. Bring to the boil and simmer gently for 45 minutes until the peas are cooked.

ADD the leeks and continue cooking for another 30 minutes until the leeks are tender.

- Serves 6
- You could garnish with extra crispy bacon or lardons.

Mushroom and lentil soup

- 1 red onion, peeled and chopped
- 2 tbsp olive oil
- 1 lemon, zested and cut into wedges
- a generous pinch of crushed chilli
- 300g mushrooms
- 6 ripe tomatoes or 400g tin tomatoes
- 1 tbsp balsamic vinegar
- 1 litres chicken stock (2 cubes)
- 450g cooked lentils (from packet or tin)
- a handful of young spinach leaves

SOFTEN the onion in the olive oil with the zest from the lemon cut into small bits, the chilli and ½ tsp salt.
IF using ripe tomatoes, pour boiling water over them and count to 30. Drain, remove the skins and chop.
STIR mushrooms and balsamic vinegar into the onion and cook, stirring, for 5 minutes. Add tomatoes and the stock. Bring to the boil, then simmer for about 15 minutes until thick. Stir in the lentils, heat through and add the spinach. When the spinach is wilted, season to taste.
GARNISH with a drizzle of olive oil and serve with a lemon wedge.

- Serves 4

Mushroom and chestnut soup

- 2 tbsp butter
- 1 onion, peeled and chopped
- 250g field mushrooms, diced
- 250g chestnut mushrooms, diced
- a slug of sherry
- 800ml chicken or vegetable stock
- 240g tin chestnuts

SOFTEN the onion in the butter over a low heat. Add the mushrooms and continue to cook until they release their juices, approx 5 mins.

ADD the sherry and stock, stir well and simmer for 10 minutes.

CHOP the chestnuts very finely in a food processor, then stir them in, reserving a few spoonfuls for garnish.

SEASON to taste before blending the soup to the texture that you like.

GARNISH with the reserved chopped chestnuts.

- Serves 4
- A rich and tasty soup.

Wild mushroom soup with goat's cheese and garlic mushroom croûtes

- 700g mixed mushrooms, sliced
- olive oil
- 30g butter
- 3 shallots, finely chopped
- 1 garlic clove, crushed
- 4 sprigs thyme
- a few dried porcini mushrooms
- 1.5 litre chicken or vegetable stock
- crème fraîche
  For the garnish:
- 100 mixed mushrooms
- 1 garlic clove, crushed
- Slices of toasted baguette
- Goat's cheese

SOAK the dried porcini mushrooms in 200ml boiling water until soft.

FRY the mixed mushrooms in 2 tbsp oil and butter until browned. Add the shallots, garlic and the thyme leaves. Season, then fry without browning until softened.

ADD the soaked mushrooms and their soaking water, discarding any grit. Pour in the stock, bring to the boil and simmer for 10 minutes. Whizz in batches until smooth, but still with a little texture. Stir in the crème fraîche and reheat before serving.

FOR the garnish, fry the mixed mushrooms in butter and garlic. Spread slices of toasted baguette with a little goat's cheese then top with the mushrooms.

- Serves 8
- Any mixture of available fresh mushrooms is good in this recipe.

Hamish Scheme 1

Warming and hearty mushroom and barley soup

- 25g pack porcini mushrooms
- 2 tbsp olive oil
- 1 medium onion, finely diced
- 2 large carrots, diced
- 2 garlic cloves, crushed
- 1 tbsp chopped rosemary
- 500g fresh mushrooms, finely chopped
- 1.2 litres vegetable stock
- 5 tbsp marsala or dry sherry
- 2 tbsp tomato purée
- 100g pearl barley

SOAK the porcini in 250ml boiling water for 25 minutes.
HEAT the oil in a saucepan and add the onion, carrot, garlic, rosemary and seasoning. Fry for 5 minutes on a medium heat until softened.
DRAIN the porcini, reserving the soaking liquid, and chop finely. Add to the pan along with the fresh mushrooms and fry for another 5 minutes.
ADD the stock, marsala or sherry, tomato purée, barley and the porcini liquid, discarding any grit.
COOK for 30 minutes or until barley is soft.
GARNISH with a sprinkling of grated parmesan.

- Serves 4–6

Chestnut mushroom soup

- 25g butter
- 1 small onion, finely chopped
- 1 garlic clove, finely chopped
- 40g plain flour
- 700ml vegetable stock
- 250g chestnut mushrooms, sliced
- 1 tbsp flat leaf parsley, finely chopped
- 75ml single cream

MELT half the butter and cook the onion and garlic gently until soft but not coloured.

STIR in the flour and cook for a further minute. Gradually add the stock, stirring all the time, until you have a thick soup.

ADD around three quarters of the mushrooms and the parsley. Cover and bring to the boil. Simmer for 10 minutes until the vegetables are tender.

COOL a little and then whizz.

MELT the remaining butter and sauté the remaining mushrooms until they begin to brown. Stir them into the soup and add the cream. Check the seasoning.

SERVE garnished with some of extra chopped parsley.

- Serves 6
- This is one of Carolyn's favourite soups.

Creamed onion soup with cider

- 5 medium onions, peeled and thinly sliced
- 1 tsp chopped thyme leaves
- 1 tbsp vegetable oil
- a generous knob butter
- 1 tbsp plain flour
- 150ml dry cider
- 1 litre vegetable stock
- 2 tbsp double cream

HEAT the oil in a large saucepan and cook the onions and thyme until soft but not brown, about 10 minutes.

ADD the butter and flour, then stir on a low heat for a minute or so, until a roux has formed.

SLOWLY add the cider, stirring constantly, then gradually add the vegetable stock and season.

BRING to the boil and simmer gently, partially covered, for 1 hour.

STIR in the cream and serve immediately.

GARNISH with a small sprig of thyme to each bowl.

- Serves 4
- 'Cheat' and use a tin of Easy Fried Onions.

Onion and cider soup with Gruyère croûtes

- 6 medium onions, halved and finely sliced
- 400g butter
- 3 garlic cloves, crushed
- 2 sprigs thyme, leaves only
- 800ml beef stock
- 568ml bottle of dry cider
- 3 tsp balsamic vinegar

FRY the onions in the butter in a large saucepan, season and leave to cook for about 30 minutes, stirring occasionally, until deeply golden, caramelised and soft.

STIR in 2 of the crushed garlic cloves and thyme sprigs. Pour in the stock, cider and vinegar, bring to a boil and simmer for about 10 minutes, spooning off any scum.

For the garnish:

BRUSH small slices of baguette on both sides with olive oil flavoured with the third garlic clove. Season and bake in a 200°C/gas mark 6 oven for about 5 minutes until toasted and crisp.

TOP each toast with a good pile of grated Gruyère (or other melty cheese).

FLOAT on top of each bowl of soup and put the bowls under a hot grill until the cheese has melted.

- Serves 6

Disappearing Diamonds by Sara

This was designed by Sara Stonor. It is a beautiful piece for the experienced stitcher. This design uses wool, Perle Cotton and Stranded Cotton and is available in four different colourways.

Caramelised onion soup

- 25g butter
- 2 medium onions
- 200g English Provender Very Lazy Caramelised Red Onions
- 2 x 415g cans beef consommé
- 400ml dry white wine
- 2 bay leaves
- 10 thyme sprigs
- 1 beef stock cube or stock pot

MELT the butter in a large saucepan, add the onions and fry over a medium heat for 8–10 minutes until softened and browned. Tip in the caramelised red onions and bubble for 2 minutes. Stir in the consommé and ½ can full of water. Bring to the boil, add the wine, the bay leaves, 4 thyme sprigs, the stock cube or pot. Simmer, uncovered, for 20 minutes or so.

For the garnish:

TOAST thin, diagonal baguette slices, then spread with butter. Mix 100g grated Gruyère and the leaves from 4 sprigs of thyme and press onto the buttered toast. Grill until the cheese is melted and golden.

LADLE the soup into warmed bowls, top with a thyme sprig and serve with a Gruyère croûte.

- Serves 6

Parsnip and Stilton soup

- 30 g butter
- 1 medium onion, roughly chopped
- 1 garlic clove, crushed
- 1 kg parsnips, roughly chopped
- 1.5 litres chicken or vegetable stock
- 1.5 tbsp sherry vinegar
- 150g Stilton, crumbled
- 140ml single cream
- vegetable crisps

MELT the butter in a large saucepan, add the onion and sweat gently until softened. Add the garlic, cook for a few minutes more and then add the parsnips and the stock. Simmer for about 20 minutes until the parsnips are tender.

REMOVE from the heat and add the vinegar and ¾ of the Stilton (save the rest for garnish).

LEAVE to cool down and then whizz until smooth. Return to the pan, season and stir in ¾ of the cream.

SERVE in warm bowls with a drizzle of cream, some of the reserved Stilton crumbled and a scattering of vegetable crisps.

- Serves 6
- The sweetness of the parsnips and the sharpness of the Stilton work well together.

Curried parsnip soup

- 40g butter or magarine
- 1 medium onion, roughly chopped
- 700g parsnips, peeled and roughly chopped
- 1 tsp curry powder or paste
- ½ tsp ground cumin
- 1.1 litres chicken stock
- 150ml single cream or milk
- paprika for garnish

MELT the butter or margarine in a large saucepan and add the onion and parsnips. Fry gently for about 5 minutes.

STIR in the curry powder or paste and cumin and cook a couple of minutes more.

ADD the stock and seasoning and bring to the boil. Simmer for about 45 minutes until the vegetables are tender.

WHIZZ until smooth. Return to the pan and check the seasoning.

ADD the cream or milk and reheat without boiling. Serve in warmed bowls sprinkled with a little paprika.

- Serves 6
- A classic warming soup.

Thick parsnip and potato soup

- 50g butter
- 4 rashers streaky bacon, chopped
- 1 onion, chopped
- 350g parsnips, peeled and chopped
- 225g potatoes, chopped
- 600ml vegetable stock
- 2 bay leaves
- 150ml milk
- 1 bunch spring onions, chopped
- 1 hanful fresh parsley, chopped

MELT the butter in a large pan, add the bacon and onion and fry gently for about 10 minutes until the bacon is crisp and the onion lightly browned.

STIR in the parsnips and potatoes. Mix well.

ADD the stock and bay leaves and bring to the boil. Reduce the heat, cover and simmer for 20–25 minutes until the vegetables are tender.

REMOVE from the heat, discard the bay leaves and purée, in batches if necessary.

RETURN the soup to the pan and stir in the milk, spring onions, parsley and seasoning. Heat through gently.

GARNISH with a dollop of yogurt in each bowl.

- Serves 4
- Fry strips of parsnip for an additional garnish.

Curried parsnip and apple soup

- 1 onion, chopped
- 1 tbsp olive oil
- 1 garlic clove, crushed
- 1 tsp ground coriander
- 1 tsp ground cumin
- 400g parsnips, peeled and diced
- 600ml vegetable stock
- 1 small Bramley apple, peeled and grated

HEAT the oil in a saucepan and cook the onion until soft. Add the garlic, coriander and cumin.

COOK for 1 minute and then add the parsnips and the vegetable stock.

COOK until the vegetables are soft.

LIQUIDISE the soup, grate in the apple. Simmer for 3 more minutes.

- Serves 2 (easily doubled)

Alhambra Scheme 1

Spicy parsnip and chorizo soup

- 100g green lentils
- 3 tbsp vegetable oil
- 1 medium chorizo, diced
- 1 large onion, chopped
- 6 parsnips, cubed
- 2 sticks celery, chopped
- 1 fresh red chilli
- 1 litre vegetable stock
- chopped fresh parsley and yogurt

COOK the lentils in salted water for about 10 minutes.

HEAT the oil in a saucepan and fry the chorizo, onion, parsnips, chilli and celery for 5 minutes.

DRAIN the lentils and add them to the pan along with the stock. Bring to the boil and then simmer until all the vegetables are tender.

CHOP the parsley and add to the yogurt. Set aside.

WHIZZ half the soup and then put the whizzed and unwhizzed parts of the soup together for a thick and chunky soup.

SERVE in warmed bowls with a spoonful of the parsleyed yogurt on top.

- Serves 4
- Remove the seeds from the chilli if you want less spiciness in the soup.

Spicy parsnip soup

- 50g butter
- 1 onion, peeled and chopped
- 500g parsnips, trimmed, peeled and chopped
- 500ml vegetable stock
- 1 tbsp runny honey
- 2 bay leaves
- a pinch each of cayenne and ground cumin
- flat leaf parsley, chopped

MELT the butter in a saucepan, add the onion and cook until soft and translucent.

ADD the parsnips, season and cook gently for 4–5 minutes. Stir in the stock, honey and bay leaves. Bring to the boil and then simmer for 20 minutes until the parsnips are tender.

DISCARD the bay leaves. Whizz until smooth. Return to the pan and stir in the cayenne and cumin. Adjust seasoning and reheat gently.

LADLE into warm bowls and garnish with the chopped flat leaf parsley.

- Serves 4
- For a garnish variation, stir the chopped parsley into some fat-free yogurt and add a dollop to the soup just before serving.

Cream of pea and asparagus soup

- 3 tbsp extra virgin olive oil
- 2 onions, finely diced
- 1 garlic clove, finely diced
- 1 litre chicken stock
- 500g frozen (or fresh) peas
- 500g trimmed asparagus, finely sliced
- 200ml double cream
- 3 tbsp chives, finely chopped

HEAT the olive oil in a large saucepan and fry the onion and garlic over a medium heat until soft and golden, about 10 minutes.

ADD the stock and bring to the boil.

ADD the peas, and as soon as they come to the boil add the asparagus and 2 tbsp of the chives.

RETURN to the simmer, cover and cook for 20 mins until very soft. Liquidise then strain.

STIR in 100ml of the double cream and adjust the seasoning to taste.

EITHER reheat or chill until needed.

MIX the remaining chives into the remaining cream and swirl into each bowl of soup as a garnish.

- Serves 8
- Equally good served hot or cold.

Pea soup with crispy bacon

- ½ tbsp olive oil
- 4 rashers smoked streaky bacon
- a knob of butter
- 4 spring onions, chopped (white & green parts)
- 600ml chicken stock
- 350g frozen petits pois
- 1 tsp mint sauce

HEAT the oil in a saucepan big enough for the soup. Cut the bacon into batons and fry until crispy. Remove from the pan and drain on kitchen paper.

ADD the knob of butter, reduce the heat and soften the spring onions.

ADD the chicken stock to the pan, bring to the boil and add the frozen petits pois. Boil for a couple of minutes until tender. Add the mint sauce.

WHIZZ until the peas have broken down and return to the pan. Check the seasoning and adjust if necessary.

SERVE in warm bowls with a dollop of crème fraîche and topped with the crispy bacon batons.

- Serves 4
- An easy but delicous soup.

Pea and mint soup

- 1 bunch spring onions, chopped
- 1 potato, chopped (no need to peel)
- 1 garlic clove, crushed
- 850ml vegetable stock
- 250g frozen peas
- a handful of mint, roughly chopped
- a pinch of sugar
- juice of 1 lemon

PUT the spring onions, potato, garlic and vegetable stock into a large saucepan. Simmer for 15 minutes. Add the frozen peas and simmer for 5 minutes more.
STIR in the mint, sugar and lemon juice.
WHIZZ until smooth.
GARNISH with a dollop of crème fraîche and a small mint leaf to each bowl.

- Serves 4
- You can use 2 medium leeks instead of spring onions.

French Canadian pea soup

- 454g dry yellow split peas
- 454g salt pork, in one piece
- 1 onion, chopped
- ½ tsp summer savory, preferably fresh
- 2 tsp salt

WASH and soak the peas according to the directions on the package. Drain and place in a large pot with 2 litres of water. Add the pork, onion and savory. Bring to a boil and simmer for 1–1½ hours, skimming any foamy layer that surfaces.

CHECK if the pork is tender and, if it is, remove it, allow it to cool and store in the fridge for another use. Continue to simmer the soup for a further 1–1½ hours.

REMOVE half the peas and purée. Return the purée to the soup, leaving the rest of the peas whole. Check for seasoning and add salt as desired.

- Serves 4 generously
- You can use winter savory instead, or if all else fails, thyme or oregano.
- French Canadian pea soup is different from American pea soup which uses a smoked ham hock.

Appleton Wools

Appleton, founded in 1835, has built up its reputation over the decades by selecting the finest English wools from the wool markets in Bradford, Yorkshire, and having them spun in the UK into either 4-ply tapestry or 2-ply crewel wool. The wool is dyed to 423 different shades, all of which are available in both tapestry and crewel weights. They can be supplied in either hanks or skeins. Appleton is particularly proud of supplying wool for the recent completion of the missing panels of the Bayeux Tapestry, among other major projects.

Roasted red pepper and sweet potato soup

- 3 sweet red peppers, seeded and chopped
- 2 sweet potatoes, peeled and cubed
- 1 onion, chopped
- 3 garlic cloves, peeled
- 25ml extra virgin olive oil
- 5ml mixed herbs
- 1 litre chicken or vegetable stock
- 150ml plain yogurt
- 25ml parsley, chopped

IN a roasting pan, toss together the red peppers, potatoes, onion, garlic, oil, mixed herbs, and season. Roast at 220°C/gas mark 7, stirring once, until tender and golden at the edges, about 45 minutes to 1 hour.

PURÉE the vegetables with the stock in batches. Strain into a saucepan.

ADD 250ml water. Bring to the boil, reduce the heat and simmer for 5 minutes.

MEANWHILE, stir the parsley into the yogurt and use to garnish.

- Serves 4
- If time is short, use a jar of roasted peppers.

Roasted pumpkin soup with chilli oil

- 900g pumpkin flesh
- olive oil
- 75g butter
- 225g onions, thinly sliced
- 750ml boiling water or light stock
- 150ml double cream
- 50g grated parmesan
- 2 tsp chilli oil

PREHEAT the oven to 200°C/gas mark 6. Remove the seeds and membranes from the pumpkin, cut off the skin and chop into chunks. Toss in a little olive oil, spread on a roasting tin and roast for about 20 minutes or until tender and starting to caramelise.

MELT the butter in a large saucepan, stir in the onions and cook gently for about 10 minutes until soft.

STIR in the roasted pumpkin, season to taste. Add the water or stock and bring to the boil. Reduce the heat and simmer gently for 30 minutes then stir in the Parmesan and the cream.

LIQUIDISE and reheat without boiling.

GARNISH with a swirl of chilli oil and a scattering of pumpkin seeds.

- Serves 6–8

Pumpkin and mascarpone soup

- 1 large onion, peeled and chopped
- 1 large knob of butter
- 2 medium-sized butternut squashes
- 2 garlic cloves, chopped
- 1.4 litres chicken stock
- 250g tub of mascarpone

HEAT the butter in a large saucepan and add the onion. Cook until soft but not coloured.

PEEL the butternut squash and remove the seeds and membranes. Cut into chunks of an even size.

ADD the squash and garlic to the onions. Stir and cook for a few minutes before adding the stock. Bring to the boil, check the seasoning and simmer for about 40 minutes or until the squash is very tender.

LIQUIDISE in batches, adding a few spoonfuls of mascarpone to each batch.

GARNISH with any of the following: croutons, fried pancetta, a dollop of crème fraîche or some chopped fresh parsley.

- Serves 8–10
- Add a tsp of garam masala at the same time as the garlic for a slightly spicy soup.
- This also works well using butternut squash.

Creamy spinach soup

- 50g butter
- 1 medium onion, finely chopped
- 2 garlic cloves, finely chopped
- 1 medium potato, peeled & chopped
- 450ml chicken or vegetable stock
- 600ml milk
- 450g fresh spinach, roughly chopped
- finely grated zest of half a lemon
- freshly grated nutmeg, to taste

MELT the butter in a large lidded saucepan, add the onion and garlic and fry gently for 5–6 minutes until softening. Stir in the potato and continue to cook gently for 1 minute. Pour in the stock and simmer for 8–10 minutes until the potato starts to cook. Pour in the milk and bring up to a simmer, then stir in half the spinach and the lemon zest. Cover and simmer for 15 minutes until the spinach has completely wilted down. Allow to cool for about 5 minutes.

LIQUIDISE and add remaining spinach (this keeps the soup bright green and fresh tasting) and process until silky smooth. You may need to do this in batches.

RETURN to the pan, reheat & add nutmeg and seasoning.

GARNISH with a swirl of cream in each bowl.

- Serves 4

Spinach and courgette soup

- oil and butter for frying
- 2 potatoes, chopped (no need to peel)
- 1 onion, chopped
- 4 garlic clovesgarlic, crushed
- 6 courgettes, chopped
- 1.5 litres vegetable stock
- a good grinding of nutmeg
- 500g spinach, washed if necessary

COOK the onion and garlic in oil and butter until soft but not coloured.

ADD the courgettes and nutmeg plus seasoning and cook a few minutes more before adding the stock. Bring to the boil and simmer a few minutes until the courgettes are tender.

ADD the spinach leaves and then remove from the heat after about 30 seconds. The spinach will wilt in the hot stock without losing its vibrant colour.

WHIZZ the soup until smooth.

- Serves 8
- You can serve this with a dollop of crème fraîche.

Spicy sweet potato and butternut squash soup

- 1 tsp each cumin, coriander and sesame seeds
- 1 tbsp light olive oil
- 1 medium onion, finely chopped
- 2 garlic cloves, crushed
- 2–3 tsp Tom Yum paste
- 1 cm fresh root ginger, peeled and finely grated
- 1 green chilli, seeded and chopped (or to taste)
- zest and juice of 1 lime
- 1 tsp runny honey
- 340g sweet potato, peeled and diced
- 340g butternut squash, peeled and diced
- 1.2 litres vegetable stock

ROAST the cumin, coriander and sesame seeds in a dry frying pan until fragrant then grind them in a spice grinder or using a pestle and mortar.

HEAT the oil and cook the onion and garlic in a covered saucepan for 10 minutes, without colouring. Add the ground seeds, Tom Yum paste, ginger, chilli, lime zest and honey and stir for 30 seconds.

ADD the sweet potato, squash, lime juice and the stock. Cover, bring to the boil and simmer for about 20 minutes.

COOL a little, then purée until very smooth.

GARNISH with a dollop of crème fraîche.

- Serves 4

Sweet potato and lentil soup

- 25g butter
- 2 tbsp olive oil
- 2 onions, peeled and chopped
- 1 medium sweet potato, peeled and chopped
- 1 medium carrot, roughly chopped
- 2 stalks celery, roughly chopped
- 150g Puy lentils (or brown lentils)
- ½ tsp turmeric
- 1 tsp ground cumin
- a pinch of ground cinnamon
- 3cm piece of fresh ginger, grated
- 3 garlic cloves, crushed
- 200g canned tomatoes
- 1 litre chicken stock
- juice of 1 lemon

COMBINE the butter and oil in a saucepan over a medium heat and sweat the onion for 10 minutes.

ADD the sweet potato, carrot, celery and lentils and stir to coat in the oil. Add all the spices, the garlic, tomatoes, stock, lemon juice and seasoning.

COOK for 30 minutes until the lentils are soft and the sweet potato is tender.

WHIZZ the soup briefly leaving it a bit chunky.

- Serves 6

Sweet potato and ginger soup

- 2 tbsp butter
- 2 red onions, peeled and finely sliced
- 1.5 tbsp fresh root ginger, grated
- 2 large sweet potatoes, peeled and chopped
- 1.5 litres chicken stock (or water)
- 150ml double cream
- 1 tbsp tamari or soya sauce (or more to taste)
- 1 tbsp maple syrup
- juice of ½ a lime, or to taste

MELT the butter in a large saucepan. Add the onions, along with a pinch of salt, and sweat gently for 5 minutes or until soft and translucent.

ADD the ginger, stir and then add the sweet potatoes and stir once more. Pour in the chicken stock and bring to the boil. Immediately reduce the heat to a simmer and cook gently for 25 minutes or until the sweet potatoes fall apart when prodded with a fork.

REMOVE from the heat and allow to cool a little. Purée in batches. Strain the soup through a fine sieve back into the pan and reheat gently.

STIR in the cream, tamari or soy sauce and maple syrup, then squeeze in the lime juice.

- Serves 6

Roasted tomato soup with basil

- 1 tbsp olive oil
- 10 large vine tomatoes, cut in half
- a few sprigs of rosemary or thyme
- 750ml chicken stock
- a handful of nice-looking basil leaves

HEAT the oven to 180°C/gas mark 4. Place the tomatoes, cut side up, on a foil lined shallow baking tray and smear with a little olive oil. Place the sprigs of herbs among the tomatoes. Roast the tomatoes with the tray on a low shelf for about an hour, until the tomatoes are slightly dried and squashy. Discard the herbs.

WHIZZ the tomatoes and their juices until good and smooth. Pour through a sieve into a clean pan to remove the pips and any bits of skin. Push the tomatoes through the sieve with the back of a wooden spoon so nothing is wasted.

ADD the chicken stock, simmer for 10 minutes and adjust the seasoning.

SERVE with a swirl of good olive oil and some torn or snipped basil leaves.

- Serves 4–6
- Roasting the tomatoes brings out their sweetness.

Morrocan Tile

This charming piece, on 14 mesh canvas, was designed by Anna Pearson. Moroccan Tile is one of our most popular kits. It is a small panel worked in a pleasing mixture of textures and colours, using crewel wool, Stranded Cotton and hand-dyed silk.

Gazpacho

- 1 kg really ripe tomatoes, roughly chopped
- 4 spring onions, chopped
- 3 garlic cloves, peeled and chopped
- ½ cucumber, peeled
- 75ml olive oil
- 2 tbsp sherry vinegar
  For the garnish:
- 2 spring onions
- ½ each red and green peppers
- 1 hard-boiled egg
- 1 slice bread

PUT the chopped tomatoes, spring onions, garlic and cucumber in a blender and whizz until smooth. Pass through a fine sieve 2 or 3 times.

PUT the mixture back in the blender and slowly add the olive oil and sherry vinegar and season well. Chill in the fridge.

TO make the garnish finely dice the spring onions, red pepper, green pepper and hard-boiled egg. Cut the bread into small cubes and gently fry in a little olive oil to make croutons.

- Serves 4–6
- Season very well, as cold food requires more seasoning than hot food.

Slow roasted tomato & red pepper soup with goat's cheese croûtes

- 4 red peppers, halved lengthways, deseeded
- 3 tbsp extra virgin olive oil
- 1 kg vine tomatoes
- 2 whole garlic bulbs
- 1 medium red onion, chopped
- 350ml vegetable stock, hot
- 1 tbsp sun-dried tomato paste
- 1 tbsp chopped fresh tarragon leaves

PREHEAT the oven to 200°C/gas mark 6. Put the peppers into a roasting tin and drizzle with 1 tbsp of the olive oil. Put the tomatoes and garlic into a separate roasting tin, season, and toss with another tbsp of the oil. Roast the peppers on the top shelf of the oven and the tomatoes and garlic on the shelf below for 25–30 minutes until the pepper skins are blistered and the garlic is soft. Transfer the peppers to a freezer bag and seal. Set aside for a few minutes to allow the skins to loosen in the steam.

HEAT the remaining oil in a large heavy-based pan, add the onion and gently fry for 5–8 minutes until soft. Squeeze the garlic flesh from the bulbs into the pan and add the tomatoes as well. Discard the skins from the peppers and add the flesh to the pan. Add the stock, sun-dried tomato paste and tarragon and bring

to the boil, then reduce the heat, cover and simmer.
ALLOW to cool a little and then whizz until roughly
puréed. Season and return to the pan. Reheat gently.
For the croûtes:
SLICE a baguette and toast one side of the slices under
a grill. Top each untoasted side with slices of goat's
cheese and season. Return to the grill until just the
cheese is just melted.
TOP each bowl of soup with a goat's cheese croûte and
a sprig of tarragon.

❖ Serves 4–6

Easy tomato soup

❖ 2 onions, chopped
❖ 2 yellow peppers, deseeded and chopped
❖ 300g mushrooms, chopped
❖ 3 tbsp mixed herbs
❖ 1 garlic clove, crushed
❖ 2 x 400g cans chopped tomatoes
❖ 500ml chicken or vegetable stock

HEAT a little oil and gently cook the onions, peppers,
mushrooms and garlic until soft.
ADD the remaining ingredients and bring to the boil.
Simmer for 5 minutes, then whizz until smooth.

❖ Serves 4–6

Watercress soup

- 6 spring onions, trimmed and sliced
- 450g potatoes, peeled and thinly sliced
- 600ml chicken or vegetable stock
- 2 x 85g bags prepared watercress
- 150ml milk
- a good grinding of nutmeg

PLACE the spring onions (you can include quite a lot of the green tops), potatoes and stock in a large saucepan and bring to the boil. Simmer until the potatoes are tender, then add the watercress, reserving a few sprigs for garnish.

SIMMER for a couple of minutes until the watercress is wilted. Season well.

ALLOW to cool slightly then whizz until smooth. Return to the pan, add the milk and nutmeg. Adjust the seasoning if necessary. Reheat until hot through.

SERVE in warmed bowls garnished with a little crème fraîche and a sprig of watercress.

- Serves 4
- This soup is equally delicious served cold.

Watercress and Wensleydale soup

- 3 tbsp olive oil
- 1 large onion, finely chopped
- 2 fat garlic cloves, chopped
- 1 celery stick, finely chopped
- 1 small carrot, finely chopped
- 350g potatoes, diced
- 1.5 litres chicken or vegetable stock
- 3 bunches of watercress, stalks removed
- 225g Wensleydale or Lancashire cheese

HEAT the oil in a large pan. Add the onion, garlic, celery and carrot and cook, stirring, for 10 minutes over a medium heat until the onion is soft but not coloured. Add the potatoes and stock, cover and simmer for 20 minutes.

SET aside a few watercress sprigs for garnish, then add the remainder to the pan. Bring to the boil and simmer for 2 mins. Cool a little then purée.

RETURN to the pan and whisk in crumbled Wensleydale or Lancashire cheese. Reheat, without boiling, then taste for seasoning.

TOP each bowl of soup with croutons, a little extra crumbled cheese and a small sprig of watercress.

- Serves 6

Summer vegetable & pesto soup

- 2 tbsp olive oil
- 1 garlic clove
- 1 onion, finely chopped
- 2 sticks celery, finely diced
- 3 courgettes, diced
- 1.5 litres vegetable stock
- 130g peas, shelled
- 100g green beans, sliced into 2cm length
- 175g broad beans, podded and skinned
- 1 tbsp each fresh basil and mint, shredded
- pesto and grated parmesan to serve

HEAT the oil in a saucepan, add the garlic, onion and celery and cook gently for 10 minutes until soft.

ADD the courgettes and stock, bring to the boil, then cover and simmer for 5 minutes.

ADD the peas, green beans, broad beans and simmer for a further 5 minutes.

REMOVE from the heat, then stir in the finely shredded fresh basil and mint.

GARNISH with grated parmesan and a dollop of fresh pesto.

- Serves 8
- You can also use frozen beans and peas if fresh vegetables are not available.

No-dice vegetable soup

- 1 onion, peeled and quartered
- 2 garlic cloves, peeled
- 2 tsp olive oil
- 1 carrot, peeled and quartered
- 1 parsnip, peeled and quartered
- 1 stick celery, quartered
- 150g broccoli florets
- 100g green beans
- 750ml tomato passata
- 750ml vegetable stock
- fresh oregano leaves

PLACE the onion and garlic in a food processor and process until roughly chopped. Place in a saucepan with the oil and cook over a medium heat for 3 minutes or until soft.

MEANWHILE place the carrot, parsnip, celery, broccoli and beans in a food processor and process until roughly chopped. Add the chopped vegetables to the saucepan along with the tomato passata and the stock and simmer for 12–15 minutes or until the vegetables are tender. Season well.

LADLE soup into bowls and sprinkle over a few oregano leaves and serve.

- Serves 4

Leftover vegetable soup

- 3 tbsp olive oil
- 1 onion, chopped
- 2 celery sticks, chopped
- 1 carrot, chopped
- 2 potatoes (approx 350g), peeled
- 1 tbsp curry powder or paste
- 1.2 litres vegetable or chicken stock
- 500g mixed leftover vegetables, chopped

HEAT the oil in a large saucepan and fry the onion, celery, carrots and potatoes until soft and golden.

STIR in the curry powder or paste, cook for a minute and then add the stock. Bring to the boil, lower the heat and simmer for about 10 minutes until the vegetables are tender. Add the leftover vegetables to the pan and heat through.

WHIZZ to a smooth purée and return to the pan. Thin to the consistency you want with water or stock and taste for seasoning.

GARNISH with a dollop of crème fraîche.

- Serves 4
- A good way to use up leftover vegatables after Christmas, Easter or just a Sunday lunch.
- Make your stock from whatever was on the menu.

Winter vegetable soup

- 1 large carrot, peeled and chopped
- 1 leek, trimmed, chopped and well rinsed
- ½ cabbage, green or white, chopped
- 1 onion, chopped
- 1 little gem lettuce, chopped
- 1 small squash or ¼ pumpkin, peeled
- 1 turnip, peeled and chopped

REMOVE the seeds from the squash or pumpkin and roughly chop.

BRING all the vegetables to the boil in a pan containing 1 litre of water. Season to taste and simmer for 25–30 minutes or until the vegetables are soft.

BLEND briefly, using either a hand-held blender or a processor, so the soup is still a little chunky. Check seasoning and adjust if necessary.

SERVE in warm bowls with a swirl of crème fraîche.

- Serves 4
- You can substitute any winter root vegetables in this recipe.

Gruyère and vegetable soup

- 1 onion
- 1 medium leek
- 1 medium carrot
- 1 small potato
- ½ bulb of fennel
- 2 tbsp olive oil
- 4 sprigs of thyme, leaves only
- 2 tbsp plain flour
- 700ml vegetable or chicken stock
- 1 small head of broccoli, cut into floretts
- handful of flat leaf parsley, roughly chopped
- 140g Gruyère, coarsely grated

PREPARE the all the vegatables: dice the onion; wash and trim the leek, cutting off and discarding half of the green top, then thinly slice; peel and chop the carrot and potato into small dice; thinly slice the fennel into bite-size sticks. The vegetables should be all roughly the same size and fit on a spoon.

HEAT the butter and oil in a medium pan and sweat all the vegetables, except the broccoli, with the thyme leaves for about 10 minutes, stirring occasionally, until softened but not brown.

ADD the flour and stir for a minute to form a roux, then slowly add the stock. Bring to the boil, stirring until thick, then add the milk, season well and simmer

for 10 minutes. Add the broccoli and cook for a further 5 minutes or until the broccoli is just tender.
Stir in most of the parsley, reserving some for garnish.
Ladle the soup into four bowls, and top with the
cheese and remaining parsley.

- Serves 4
- You can use a stalk of celery instead of the
  half a bulb of fennel.

Fiona Scheme IV

Root vegetable and barley soup

- 1 kg root vegetables
- 1 onion
- 1 stick celery
- 30g butter
- 1.5 litres vegetable or chicken stock
- 150g pearl barley
- 1 tbsp chopped fresh thyme

PEEL and dice your mixed root vegetables (carrots, celeriac, parsnips, swede and/or leeks). Chop the onion and celery.

GENTLY fry all the vegetables in the butter in a large pan for about 5 minutes.

ADD the stock, thyme and the barley, and bring to boil. Simmer for approx 35 minutes until everything is tender.

SERVE with garnished with chopped parsley, a swirl of cream or crumbled fried streaky bacon.

- Serves 6
- The addition of barley makes this a really rich and filling soup.

Pistou

- 2 tbsp olive oil
- 1 onion, chopped
- 2 spring onions, chopped
- 2 garlic cloves, crushed
- 1.2 litres vegetable stock
- 250g baby new potatoes, halved or quartered
- 250g Chantenay carrots, halved if large
- 170g fine beans, chopped into short lengths
- 2 courgettes, diced
- 8 ripe tomatoes, skinned and chopped
- 500g broad beans, podded, cooked & skinned
- 400g petits pois (frozen is fine)
- a jar of green pesto

HEAT the oil and fry the onion, spring onions and garlic in a large saucepan until soft but not coloured.

ADD the stock and potatoes. Cook for 10 minutes.

ADD the carrots, green beans, courgettes, tomatoes and cook 8–10 minutes. Check the amount of liquid and add some water if necessary.

ADD the broad beans and peas. Simmer a further 5 minutes. Season and add 3 tbsp of pesto.

SERVE in warmed bowls with a dollop of pesto on each bowl.

- Serves 8 generously

Hand-Painted Canvas "Eryngium"

Our hand painted canvasses are done for us by Sarah Blackett-Ord, a Northumbrian artist. All the colours Sarah uses are specifically matched to Appleton Wool colours.

Sarah's paintings are of plants and flowers, architectural features, buildings and still life. She works in watercolour but also used oil, pencil, crayon and ink.

Pulses and Pasta Soups

❖❖❖❖❖❖❖❖❖❖❖❖❖

White bean soup with chorizo and rosemary

- ❖ 2 tbsp olive oil
- ❖ 2 onions, diced
- ❖ 2 celery stalks, diced
- ❖ 2 carrots, diced
- ❖ 4 garlic cloves, crushed
- ❖ 2 sprigs of rosemary
- ❖ 2 x 400g tins cannellini beans
- ❖ 1 litre chicken or vegetable stock
- ❖ 2 tbsp single cream
- ❖ 8 slices Spanish chorizo, cut into matchsticks

HEAT the oil in a large saucepan. Add the onion, celery and carrot and sweat for 10 minutes until softened. Add the garlic and rosemary and cook, stirring for another 2 minutes.

DRAIN and rinse the beans, add them to the pan with the stock and simmer for 10 minutes. Cool a little, discard the rosemary and whizz until smooth with the cream. Return to the pan, reheat and check the seasoning.

HEAT a small frying pan over a medium heat, add the chorizo and fry until it realeases its oil.

DIVIDE into four bowls and scatter some of the fried chorizo along with some of the oil that was released.

- ❖ Serves 4

Bean soup (minestra di fagioli)

- 225g dried white haricot beans
- 1.7 litres chicken stock
- 2 garlic cloves, chopped
- 3 tbsp flat leaf parsley, chopped
- extra virgin olive oil

SOAK the beans overnight in water. The next day, drain the soaked beans and rinse well in several changes of fresh cold water. Place in a large saucepan and cover with stock (or water) and bring to the boil. Simmer for 2–2½ hours, watching that the liquid does not evaporate too quickly, until the beans are tender.

DRAIN the beans, reserving a some of the cooking liquid. Whizz, adding enough of the cooking liquid to make a purée. Return to the pan and season.

FRY the garlic in 2 tbsp of the oil until soft but not coloured. Stir in the parsley. Add this mixture to the soup and check the seasoning.

SERVE in warmed bowls with a drizzle of extra virgin olive oil on each bowl.

- Serves 4
- Easy to make and simply delicious.

Winter minestrone

- 2 tbsp olive oil
- 2 medium carrots, roughly chopped
- 1 large red onion, coarsely chopped
- 1 bunch celery, chopped (reserve the leaves)
- 1 head of garlic, cloves peeled
- 1kg Swiss chard
- 1 kg cavolo nero or kale
- a bunch of parsley, finely chopped
- 400g tin peeled plum tomatoes
- 410g tin cannellini beans, drained and rinsed
- 700ml chicken or vegetable stock
- winter herbs (thyme or sage), chopped

HEAT the olive oil in a large saucepan and slowly fry the carrots, onion and celery until soft and dark. This will take about 20 minutes.

SHRED the chard and cavolo nero or kale leaves, and roughly chop the stems.

ADD the garlic, chard stalks and half the parsley to the saucepan and stir to prevent sticking.

STIR in the tomatoes and cook for 10 minutes until reduced a bit.

ADD half the shredded chard leaves, half the cavolo nero (or kale) leaves, three-quarters of the beans and the boiling stock. Bring to the boil then reduce the heat and simmer for 30 minutes. Add more stock if you think it is too thick but not too much as the soup should be thick.

ADD the remaining chard and cavolo nero (or kale) leaves and blanch briefly so they remain green and crisp. Season when slightly cooled.

PUREE the remaining cannellini beans coarsely in a blender with some of the cooking liquid. Add to the soup—it should be very green. Stir in the herbs.

SERVE garnished grated parmesan and a drizzle of extra virgin olive oil.

❖ Serves 4

Harriet Scheme IV

Minestrone with salsa verde and cheese toasts

- 3 tbsp olive oil
- 2 medium red onions, diced
- 4 medium carrots, diced
- 2 celery sticks, diced
- 3 garlic cloves, crushed
- 3 sprigs each thyme & rosemary, leaves only
- 1.2 litres hot vegetable stock
- 400g can plum tomatoes
- 2 tbsp tomato purée
- 410g can cannellini beans, drained and rinsed
- 1 leek, thinly sliced

HEAT the olive oil in a large saucepan and cook the *soffrito* (onions, carrots and celery) over a medium heat for about 8 minutes without colouring until soft. Stir in the garlic, rosemary and thyme and cook gently a few minutes more.

POUR in the hot stock and bring to the boil. Simmer for 8 minutes or so. Stir in the plum tomatoes, breaking them up, the tomato purée and the beans. Simmer until cooked through, about 10 minutes.

For the salsa verde:

MIX together a crushed garlic clove, 1 tbsp olive oil, 2 tbps red wine vinegar and 45g chopped fresh flat leaf parsley. Chill until required.

WHEN ready to serve, heat the soup gently. Stir in the sliced leek and cook a few minutes to soften.

For the cheese toasts:

LIGHTLY toast 4 slices of crusty bread, sprinkle with the grated ewe's cheese and grill until the cheese is bubbling. Slice into soldiers.

SERVE the soup in warmed bowls with a little salsa verde on spooned on top of each bowl.

❖ Serves 6

Butter bean and sun-dried tomato soup

- ❖ 2 x 400g cans butter beans
- ❖ 900ml vegetable stock
- ❖ 60ml sun-dried tomato paste
- ❖ 75ml pesto

DRAIN beans and put in a saucepan with the vegetable stock. Bring to the boil.

STIR in the tomato paste and pesto and simmer for 5 minutes. Whizz to a smooth liquid.

SERVE in warm bowls topped with a dollop of crème fraîche and some chopped parsley.

❖ Serves 4

DMC Perle and Stranded Cottons

We use DMC threads, which are world-renowned for their vividness of colour and quality, in our kits. DMC's Stranded Cotton (below) is available in 465 brilliant colours. DMC Perle Cotton thread (above) is a non-divisible thread with a silky shine and satin finish. It comes in different thicknesses, and the most popular size (5) is available in 309 shades.

Chickpea and chorizo soup

- 2 x 400g cans chopped tomatoes
- 250g chorizo (whole, not sliced)
- a small Savoy cabbage
- a pinch of chilli flakes
- 2 x 410g chickpeas, drained and rinsed
- 2 chicken or vegetable stock cubes

PUT a medium pan on the heat and tip in the cans of tomatoes and add 2 cans of water.

WHILE the tomatoes are heating up, chop the chorizo into chunks removing any skin. Shred the cabbage, discarding any tough stalks.

ADD the chorizo and the cabbage to the pan with the chilli flakes and chickpeas, then crumble in the stock cube. Stir well, cover and leave to cook on a high heat for about 5 minutes until the cabbage is cooked.

LADLE into bowls and serve with crusty bread.

- Serves 4
- This recipe is also very nice with kale instead of Savoy cabbage.

Indian chickpea soup

- 2 tbsp vegetable oil
- 2 red onions, finely sliced
- 2 garlic cloves, crushed
- 1 tsp curry powder
- ½ tsp dried chilli
- 1 tbsp brown mustard seeds
- 1 tsp ground turmeric
- 400ml coconut milk
- 850ml chicken or vegetable stock
- 2 x 400g cans chickpeas, drained and rinsed
- 300g baby spinach leaved, shredded

COOK the onions in a large saucepan with the oil over medium heat for about 5 minutes. Reduce the heat to low, cover and cook for a further 10 minutes. The onions should be very soft and a dark golden colour. Add the garlic and cook for a further 2–3 minutes.

ADD the curry powder, chilli, mustard seeds and turmeric and stir until the spices release their flavour, a couple of minutes. Add the coconut milk, the stock and the chickpeas and bring to the boil. Reduce the heat and simmer for 10 minutes.

ADD the spinach before serving and cook until it is wilted. Season and serve with warm Indian flatbread.

- Serves 4

Moroccan chickpea soup

- 1 tbsp olive oil
- 1 onion, chopped
- 2 sticks of celery
- 2 tsp ground cumin
- 600ml hot vegetable stock
- 400g can chopped plum tomatoes with garlic
- 400g can chickpeas, drained and rinsed
- 100g frozen broad beans
- zest and juice of ½ a lemon
- large handful of parsley, chopped

HEAT the oil in a large saucepan then fry the onion and celery for 8–10 minutes until softened, stirring frequently. Add the cumin and cook for a further minute.

TURN up the heat and add the stock, tomatoes and chickpeas and a good grinding of black pepper. Simmer for 8 minutes. Add the broad beans and lemon juice and cook for a further 2 minutes.

SEASON to taste, then top with a sprinkling of lemon zest and chopped parsley.

SERVE with flatbreads.

- Serves 4
- You can substitute frozen soy beans for the frozen broad beans.

Spiced lentil and ginger soup

- ❖ olive oil
- ❖ 1 medium onion, finely chopped
- ❖ 1 large carrot, peeled and diced
- ❖ 2 sticks celery, finely chopped
- ❖ 25g ginger, grated
- ❖ 2 garlic cloves, crushed
- ❖ 1 red chilli, finely sliced
- ❖ 1 tbsp medium curry powder
- ❖ 150g red lentils, rinsed
- ❖ 400g can chopped tomatoes

HEAT the oil in a large saucepan and fry the onion, carrot and celery for about 5 minutes. Add the ginger, garlic and chilli. Remove the seeds from the chilli if you don't want the soup to be so hot. Cook 2 minutes more.

STIR in the curry powder and a splash or two of cold water. Cook a couple of minutes stirring all the time. Add the lentils and tomatoes. Add 3 cans of water to the pan.

SEASON then bring to the boil. Simmer for about half an hour or until the lentils are tender and the soup has thickened.

SERVE with a swirl of yogurt in each bowl.

- ❖ Serves 4

Lentil, bacon and potato soup

- 1 tbsp olive oil
- 1 onion, chopped
- 6 rashers smoked streaky bacon, chopped
- 175g baby leeks, rinsed and chopped
- 400g potatoes, peeled and diced
- 1 tbsp fresh thyme, chopped
- 1.5 litres vegetable stock
- 410g tin green lentils

HEAT the olive oil in a saucepan and fry the chopped onion and bacon for a few minutes until tender but not brown.

ADD the chopped leeks and cook for a further few minutes.

ADD the diced potatoes, chopped thyme and the vegetable stock. Bring to a boil, reduce to a simmer and cook for about 20 minutes until the potatoes are tender. Add the drained lentils for the final 5 minutes of cooking.

YOU can crush the potatoes in the pan using the back of a wooden spoon or a potato masher or leave it all whole as you like. Check the seasoning and serve.

- Serves 6
- This recipe freezes well.

Puy lentil, spinach and bacon soup

- 200g Puy lentils
- 1 tbsp olive oil
- 140g unsmoked lardons
- 2 red onions, chopped
- 4 garlic cloves, chopped
- 500g fresh tomatoes, skinned and chopped
- 150ml white wine
- 400g baby spinach
- 500ml chicken or vegetable stock
- handful of chopped fresh parsley

BRING a large pan of water to the boil, add the lentils and simmer for 20–30 minutes until tender, then drain them and set aside.

FRY the bacon in the oil until golden, stirring occasionally. Transfer to a bowl using a slotted spoon and leaving the fat in the pan.

ADD the onions to the pan and sweat for 10 minutes until softened and slightly coloured. Add the garlic and cook for a couple of minutes. Then return the bacon to the pan.

STIR in the tomatoes and cook until they collapse. Add the wine and cook until it is reduced by half.

ADD the spinach and cook until it wilts. Stir in the

cooked lentils, add the stock and season well. Bring to the boil and stir in the parsley just before serving.

- ❖ Serves 6
- ❖ To skin tomatoes easily, cut a cross in the base of each tomato, just through the skin. Pour a kettle of boiling water over them, leave them for half a minute and then drain. Plunge them into cold water and when cool enough to handle, slip the skins off.

Fez Scheme II

Quick minestrone with tortellini

- olive oil
- 1 medium onion, chopped
- 2 garlic cloves, crushed
- a pinch of chilli flakes
- 2 stalks of celery, chopped
- 1 medium carrot, peeled and diced
- small bunch parsley, chopped
- 1 courgette, diced
- 400g tin chopped tomatoes
- 500ml vegetable stock
- 250g pack of cheese tortellini

HEAT 1 tbsp olive oil in a saucepan and add the onion, GARLIC, some seasoning and the chilli flakes.
COOK for 5 minutes then add the celery, carrot, the courgette and half the parsley. Fry for 5 minutes more. Tip in the tomatoes and break up slightly. Add the stock and simmer for 10 minutes.
COOK the tortellini in a separate saucepan, following the pack instructions. Add to the soup and stir well.
GARNISH with a sprinkling of chopped parsley.

- Serves 2
- You can substitute any pasta for the tortellini.

Orzo, bacon and lentil soup

- 200g smoked lardons
- 1 onion, chopped
- 2 garlic cloves, chopped
- 1 celery stalk, chopped
- 1 carrot, diced
- 2 tomatoes, peeled and chopped
- 200g green lentils
- 1.5 litres chicken stock
- 100g orzo
- handful flatleaf parsley, chopped

COOK the lardons, onion, garlic, celery and carrot in a large saucepan for around 5 minutes until the lardons start to get crisp. You won't need any oil.

ADD the tomatoes and cook for a couple of minutes until pulpy then stir in the lentils and stock. Bring to the boil, cover and simmer for 15 minutes.

ADD the orzo pasta and cook for a further 8 minutes (or whatever time it says on the packet).

- Serves 4
- If you want to prepare this soup in advance, do not add the orzo. When you ready to serve the soup, reheat it, add the orzo and cook for the recommended time.

Shotley by Shelagh

This Florentine tapestry was designed by Shelagh Martell. This is worked in crewel wools on 14 mesh canvas. It is suitable for less experienced stitchers and is a very good design for upholstery projects. It can be stitched to any size.

Game, Fish and Fowl Soups

✖✖✖✖✖✖✖✖✖✖✖✖✖✖

Game and lentil soup

- 75g butter
- 4 rabbit shoulders, or pheasant legs, pigeons or other game (not too high)
- 1 onion, sliced coarsely
- 2 carrots, sliced coarsely
- 2 celery sticks, sliced coarsely
- 750g game carcasses
- 1 heaped tbsp plain flour
- 1 litre chicken stock or water
- bouquet garni (or a Knorr herb infusion pot)
- 300g green Puy lentils
- 200g potatoes, peeled and cubed

MELT the butter in a heavy casserole dish and colour the pieces of game gently on all sides, then remove to a plate.

ADD the onion, carrots and celery to thecasserole and cook them gently for 5 minutes. Add carcasses to the pot, and cook for 3–4 minutes so they get some colour. Sprinkle over the flour, ½ tsp salt and a good grinding of black pepper. Stir well so that the fat is absorbed then add the stock or water.

RETURN the pieces of game to the pot, with the bouquet garni or the herb infusion pot and bring to the boil. Skim any scum off the surface and simmer over a very low heat for 1–1½ hours. Put the potato cubes and the Puy lentils in a separate pan. Cover with cold water, bring to the boil and simmer for 25 minutes or until the lentils are tender.

CAREFULLY lift out the game pieces and strip the meat from the bones, adding the meat to the pot of lentils. Remove the carcasses and strain the rest of the stock, pushing it through a fine sieve with the back of a wooden spoon.

ADD the stock to the pot of lentils, potato and meat, bring to the boil and simmer for a further 10 minutes.

COOL slightly and then liquidise to a really smooth purée. Pass it through a sieve if you are in doubt about the smoothness. Taste for seasoning, adding a little lemon juice if you think the taste needs lifting.

SERVE with croutons.

❖ Serves 6

Izmir Scheme I

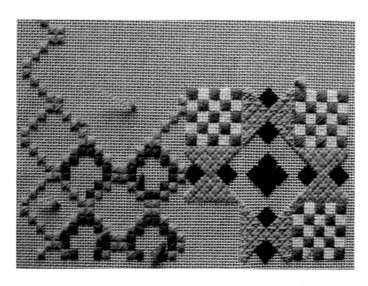

Tiles of St Mark

This image shows a part-stitched canvas of Tiles of St Mark. This is a design by Anna Pearson on 14 mesh canvas inspired by the tile patterns on the floor of St Mark's Basilica in Venice. Parts of this design were used for the specially stitched front cover of this cookbook. All our kits include detailed instructions and charts.

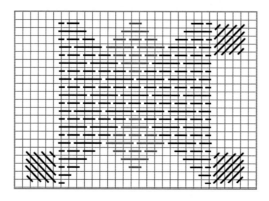

Spicy pheasant soup

- 40g butter
- 1 red pepper, seeded and chopped
- 1 onion, chopped
- 25g flour
- 1 tbsp tomato purée
- 400g can chopped tomatoes
- bouquet garni (or a Knorr herb infusion pot)
- 1.1 litres pheasant stock
- ½ tsp cayenne pepper
- ½ tsp paprika
- ¼ tsp sugar
- 1 tsp vinegar
- 2 tsp grated (not creamed) horseradish
- 175g cooked pheasant, minced

MELT the butter in a large saucepan and cook the pepper and onion until soft. Add the flour and cook for about 1 minute.

STIR in the tomato purée, canned tomatoes, bouquet garni (or herb infusion pot) and seasoning. Simmer for 30 minutes.

REMOVE the bouquet garni, if using, and add the remaining ingredients. Cook for a further 3 minutes.

SERVE in warmed bowls with crusty bread.

- Serves 4–6

Smoked haddock and potato soup

- 4 garlic cloves, peeled and sliced
- 2 medium onions, peeled and diced
- 2 medium leeks, washed and sliced
- 2 potatoes, peeled and diced
- a pinch of saffron threads
- 50g butter
- 1 litre fish stock
- 400g smoked haddock, skinned and diced
- handful of parsley, chopped
- zest and juice of 1 lemon

SWEAT the garlic, onions, leeks, potatoes and saffron in the butter with 1 tsp salt and 2 tbsp water for 6 minutes.

POUR over the stock, bring to the boil and simmer for 5 minutes or until the potatoes are tender.

ADD the haddock, turn down the heat and poach for 5 minutes. Stir in the chopped parsley, the lemon zest and juice. Season and serve.

- Serves 4
- Undyed smoked haddock works best in this.

Smoked haddock and spinach soup with mint

- olive oil
- 1 onion, sliced
- 1 potato, chopped
- 1.5 litres vegetable stock
- 300g undyed smoked haddock fillet
- large handful of mint leaves
- 300g young leaf spinach

HEAT 1 tbsp olive oil in a pan and cook the onion until soft. Add the potato along with 1 litre of stock. Bring to the boil and simmer for about 15 minutes until the potato is soft.

LAY the haddock fillet, skin-side up, on the surface of the stock and simmer very gently for about 6–8 minutes. Lift out of the pan and peel off the skin.

ADD the mint and spinach to the pan. Stir together for 30 seconds then liquidise until smooth. Return to the pan and add the rest of the stock gradually until the soup has the consistency of single cream. Flake the fish into large chunks and add to the soup, reserving some for garnish. Reheat gently and season.

SERVE scattered with the remaining flakes of fish and a dollop of crème fraîche.

- Serves 4

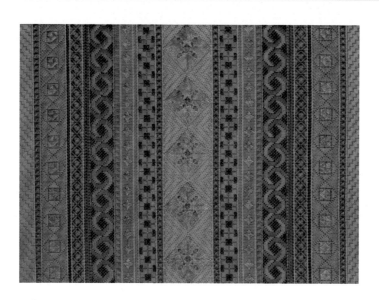

Calabria by Valerie

Valerie Hand is an extremely experienced stitcher who prefers to work on 18 mesh. This is a very decorative panel using Stranded Cottons, Perle Cottons and silk. This design has been worked as a table runner by repeating the entire design four times lengthways. It looks stunning. It is our best-selling design on 18 mesh canvas.

Smoked cod and prawn chowder

- 1 bay leaf
- 500g naturally smoked cod
- 25g butter
- 1 medium onion, chopped
- 1 garlic clove, chopped
- 225g potatoes, peeled and cut into small cubes
- 1 tbsp plain flour
- 150ml white wine
- 300ml milk
- 120ml cream
- 220g prawns, peeled
- 280g sweetcorn
- handful fresh parsley, chopped

COOK the fish in water with the bay leaf until it flakes. Drain the fish, reserving 200ml of the stock.

MELT the butter in another large saucepan and fry the onion for 5 minutes until soft. Add the garlic and potatoes and cook a few minutes more. Add the flour, then stir in the white wine and simmer for 2 minutes.

STIR in the reserved fish stock and the milk. Simmer gently for 5 minutes.

STIR through the cream, poached cod, prawns, sweetcorn and parsley. Simmer to heat through.

- Serves 4

21st Century Yarns

Another supplier of specialist yarns for our kits is 21st Century Yarns, a UK company based in Oxfordshire. They specialise in hand-dyed silks (pictured above), Stranded Cottons and wools in a wonderful array of colours and textures.

Chunky chicken and ham chowder

- 1 tbsp sunflower oil
- 2 leeks, thinly sliced
- 2 large potatoes, cut into small cubes
- 1 tbsp plain flour
- 700ml skimmed milk
- 2 ready-roasted chicken breasts
- 2 thick slices of ham, chopped
- 175g frozen sweetcorn
- 175g frozen peas

HEAT the oil in a large pan and fry the leeks over a low heat for 3 minutes until softened. Stir in the potatoes and flour, then slowly blend in the milk, stirring constantly.

BRING to the boil and simmer, uncovered, for 10–12 minutes until the potatoes are soft.

REMOVE the skin from the chicken breasts and cut into chunks. Add the chicken, ham, sweetcorn and peas, then stir over a medium heat for 5 minutes or until hot and bubbling. Season to taste.

SERVE with crusty bread.

- Serves 4
- You can use 3 pheasant breasts instead of the chicken breasts

Spiced chicken soup with vegetables, coconut and ginger

- 2 tbsp vegetable oil
- 1 garlic clove, crushed
- 3cm piece of fresh ginger, grated
- 1 red chilli, finely chopped
- 6–7 spring onions, finely sliced
- 1 red pepper, deseeded and finely sliced
- 1 orange pepper, deseeded and finely sliced
- 5 carrots, peeled and very finely sliced
- 2 celery sticks, very finely sliced
- 400ml can coconut milk
- 750ml vegetable stock
- 1 tbsp tomato purée
- 500g cooked chicken, sliced
- a squeeze of lime juice
- a splash of Thai fish sauce
- handful fresh coriander or parsley, chopped
- handful sugar snap peas, sliced lengthways
- chilli oil and lime wedges to serve

MAKE sure that the slices of the vegetables and chicken are short enough to fit on a spoon otherwise it is impossible to eat! Keep the green parts of the sliced spring onion to one side.

HEAT the oil in a large pan over a high heat. Briefly

stir-fry the garlic, ginger, chilli and the white parts of the spring onions.

NEXT add the peppers, carrots, celery, coconut milk and stock. Stir in the tomato purée and add the chicken. Cover and bring to the boil. Simmer for 6–8 minutes until the vegetables are tender and the chicken is heated through.

SEASON with the lime juice, the fish sauce and the coriander or parsley.

ADD the sugar snap peas and the green parts of the spring onion. Simmer until just cooked.

LADLE into bowls and drizzle with a little chilli oil. Serve with lime wedges on the side.

❖ Serves 6

Ragtime Scheme I

Millfield stitched by Carolyn

Carolyn Dowie adapted this design by Sheila Stainton.
A decorative small piece worked in mixed threads on
14 mesh canvas, it is available in four colourways.

Breads

✧ ✧ ✧ ✧ ✧ ✧ ✧ ✧ ✧ ✧ ✧ ✧ ✧ ✧

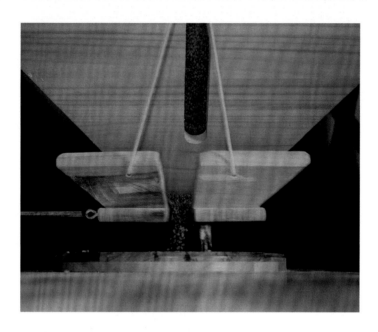

Gilchesters Organics

Gilchesters Organics is the only commercial and organic flour mill in the North East of England. Their mill, which has been operating since 2006, is situated just north of Hadrian's Wall at Gilchesters Farm. There they grow and stone-grind their heritage organic flours. These include their wholemeal flours, a light brown farmhouse, an unbleached white and a refined pizza and ciabatta white wheat flour. Pictured above is their mill at work, processing grains for their specialist flours used in our bread recipes.

Feta and sun blush tomato bread

- 500g Gilchesters unbleached white flour
- 2 tsp salt
- 7g dried yeast or 20g fresh yeast
- 1 tsp honey
- 200ml warm water
- 150ml lukewarm milk
- 250g feta cheese, cubed
- 100g sun blush tomatoes, drained

DISSOLVE the yeast and honey in about a third of the warm water in a bowl. Add 2 tbsp of flour and stir well. Leave in a warm place for 10–15 minutes to froth up.

ADD the bubbly mixture to the rest of the flour and gradually add the remaining water.

KNEAD well for about 10 minutes, either by hand or using a food processor. Put in a large oiled bowl and cover with a tea towel. Leave in a warm place for about 30 minutes until doubled in size.

KNOCK back the dough and knead in the cheese and tomatoes. Shape into two oblong loaves or a number of rolls and place on a floured baking sheet. Cover and leave in a warm place until well risen.

PREHEAT oven to 220°C/gas mark 7.

BRUSH the top with a little oil reserved from the sun blush tomatoes and bake for 25–30 minutes for loaves and 15–20 minutes for rolls.

Filled foccacia

- 15g fresh yeast or 7g dried yeast
- 275ml warm water
- 500g Gilchesters unbleached white flour
- 1.5 tsp salt
- 3 tbsp olive oil
- rosemary sprigs and coarse sea salt

DUST a large flat baking tray with flour.

PUT the flour into a bowl and add the salt. Dissolve the yeast in a little warm water. Make a soft but not sticky dough with the flour, oil, salt and yeast mixture, adding more water if necessary.

KNEAD for 10 minutes by hand on a lightly floured surface or 5 minutes with a dough hook.

SHAPE the dough into an oval and put it on the baking tray. Flatten it out to about 30cm long and 20cm wide. Cover the dough loosely with oiled clingfilm and leave to rise for about an hour or until it has doubled in size.

PREHEAT the oven to 220°C/gas mark 7. Press deep holes in the risen dough with your floured finger at regular intervals. Cut 3cm sprigs of the rosemary and push them into the holes. Sprinkle with sea salt and bake for about 25 to 30 minutes or until the bread is well risen and pale golden-brown.

REMOVE from the oven, drizzle with olive oil and leave to cool on the baking tray.

Spelt soda bread

- 300g Gilchesters wholemeal spelt flour
- 5g Maldon sea salt
- 10g baking soda
- 5g baking powder
- 1 tbsp molasses
- 230ml buttermilk

PREHEAT oven to 230°C/gas mark 8. Line a baking tray with baking paper or oil it and sprinkle with semolina to avoid the bread sticking to the tray.

MIX all dry ingredients in a bowl. Add the buttermilk and molasses and, using a scraper, mix the ingredients quickly together for about 2 minutes. The moment all the ingredients have mixed together and you have a sticky dough, flour your work surface and tip the dough onto it. Then cupping the dough between your floury hands shape it into a round dome and place on your baking tray.

USING a wooden spoon, cut a cross deeply into the dough, sprinkle some flour on top and bake for 15–20 minutes until your Spelt Soda Bread has a golden crust and sounds hollow when tapped on the bottom LEAVE to cool completely.

Olive and pesto ciabatta

Long slow fermentation brings out the flavour of light flours and makes bread more digestible. Using a 'sponge' enables you to start with a small amount of yeast which grows overnight. Natural acids that build up in the sponge help make a stretchy, open-textured dough.

Overnight sponge:
- 125g Gilchesters ciabatta flour
- 125 g water (at about 15°C)
- 7g fresh yeast (5g dried)

The dough:
- 250g overnight sponge
- 275g Gilchesters ciabatta flour
- 10ml extra virgin olive oil
- 5g salt
- 150ml warm water (approx)
- 150g pitted black olives
- 50g green pesto

FOR the sponge, dissolve the yeast in the water, add the flour and mix. Leave at room temperature to ferment for 16–24 hours.

MIX the overnight sponge, flour, oil, salt and water together. The dough should be very wet and sticky. Knead by hand or in a mixer until you have achieved a springiness and natural elasticity in the dough. Do not add any more flour, even though the dough seems impossibly soft. Now work in the olives and pesto, leaving the dough slightly streaky.

PUT the dough on a dampened area of work bench and cover it with an upturned bowl.

ONCE you have seen that the dough has risen appreciably, remove the bowl. Dust the dough and the worktop next to it with flour. Using a plastic scraper or something similar carefully cut the dough into three roughly equal pieces. As you cut, flour the incision to prevent the surfaces from rejoining.

TAKE each piece of dough and very gently—trying not to deflate the air bubbles that have formed in the dough—place it on a baking tray. Dusted with flour, stretch it longways, and form it into its characteristic 'slipper' shape. Give the finished pieces a final dusting of flour and then cover them for a final proof (1–2 hours) which should see their volume double.

BAKE in a hot oven 220°C/gas mark 8 for 12–15 minutes. Ciabatta should be only lightly brown because the floured surface prevents the crust from taking colour or going crusty.

Recipe courtesy of Andrew Whitley. His book *Bread Matters* contains many other recipes that work well with Gilchesters Organic flour. For more information, go to *www.breadmatters.com*.

Maltese Tile by Jane

Designed by Jane Allen, based on a larger design by Anna Pearson which was called 'India'. This decorative small panel has numerous different stitches worked in crewel wool, hand-dyed silk and Stranded Cotton. A good size to take away on holiday.

Soda bread from Grizel Stewart

- 100g self-raising flour
- 225g Granary or wholemeal flour
- 1 tsp bicarbonate of soda
- 1 tsp cream of tartar
- pinch of salt
- 1 tbsp clear honey or sugar
- 285ml milk
- handful of pumpkin seeds or mixed seeds

STIR all ingredients together and put into a 2lb loaf tin. Scatter the top with seeds. Cover with oiled tin foil. COOK 35 mins at 180°C/gas mark 4 or the middle of Aga, bottom right. Remove foil for last 5 minutes or until top is brown and the sides are coming away from the tin.

Bread machine malted brown loaf

- ¾ tsp dried yeast
- 250g strong granary flour
- 150g strong white flour
- 1 tsp sugar
- 15g butter
- 1 tsp salt
- 280ml water

BAKE at whole wheat setting (medium).

Networkers and Classes

Hexham, Northumberland
- ❖ Carolyn Dowie and Shelagh Martell
- ❖ carolyn.dowie@btopenworld.com

Edinburgh, Scotland
- ❖ Carolyn Dowie
- ❖ carolyn.dowie@btopenworld.com

Piercebridge, Yorkshire
- ❖ Shelagh Martell
- ❖ lalla@martellhq.com

Robertsbridge, Sussex
- ❖ Sara Stonor
- ❖ sara@stonor.org.uk

Chiddingfold, Surrey
- ❖ Jane Allen
- ❖ jane.allen01@talktalk.net

Northleach, Gloucestershire
- ❖ Valerie Hand
- ❖ valeriemhand@yahoo.co.uk

Primrose Hill, London
- ❖ Anna Pearson
- ❖ anna.pearson@tesco.net

For information about becoming a networker
- ❖ Carolyn Dowie: 01434 672 389

Useful Contacts

Appletons Wool Ltd
- www.appletons.org.uk
- sales@appletons.org.uk

21st Century Yarns
- www.21stcenturyyarns.com
- info@21stcenturyyarns.com

DMC
- www.dmccreative.co.uk
- sales@dmccreative.co.uk

Sarah Blackett-Ord
- www.sarahblackettord.com
- sbord@onetel.com

Anna Pearson
- anna.pearson@tesco.net

Gilchesters Organics
- www.gilchesters.com
- info@gilchesters.com

Andrew Whitley
- www.breadmatters.com
- info@breadmatters.com

All Stitched Up
- www.needle-point.co.uk
- 01434 672 389

Index